T0151473

Surfaces and Masks

A POEM BY CLARENCE MAJOR

COFFEE HOUSE PRESS :: MINNEAPOLIS :: 1988

This project is supported in part by The National Endowment for the Arts, a federal agency; Star Tribune/Cowles Media Company, and United Arts. The publishers also thank Minnesota Center for Book Arts, where Coffee House has been a Visiting Press since 1985.

Coffee House Press books are available to the trade through our distributor: Consortium Book Sales and Distribution, 213 East Fourth Street, Saint Paul, Minnesota 55101. Our books are also available through all major library distributors and jobbers, and through most small press distributors, including Bookpeople, Bookslinger, Inland, Pacific Pipeline, and Small Press Distribution. For personal orders, catalogs, or other information, write to: Coffee House Press, Post Office Box 10870, Minneapolis, Minnesota 55458.

Library of Congress Cataloging in Publication Data

Major, Clarence.
    Surfaces and masks : a poem / by Clarence Major
        p. cm.
    ISBN 0-918273-43-9 (pbk. : alk. paper) : $8.95
    1. Venice (Italy) — Poetry. I. Title.
PS3563.A39S87 1988
811'.54 — dc 19   88-23673
                        CIP

Surfaces And Masks

I

and who must remain
    stuck with the idea
that the Byzantine is "unlovely"
        or with the notion that
a "cultivated Negro" is necessary in a country
where one does not expect to find him,
                  available
and speaking many languages, causing one to
feel ignorant?
        Had he been a son of North Africa
and not South Carolina — what then?
This Beloved Humorist
        on the one hand
could damn the Arabs
and defend the rights of Negroes;
step into Santa Maria dei Frari
        and feel outrage
in the entranceway. And why

was the gondola black?
Behind every closed window
on the Grand Canal, Othello and Desdemona.
The threat of cholera, then
        hung like fog on the surface
of the page, in the end being itself
a signal
        vast signs of poverty, many
beggars begging — insisting really
    on their own serious anger . . .

Thomas Mann. Thomas Mann
    was impatient with the closed windows,

the smelly streets,
              did not imagine Desdemona
but a boy white-shod, "at once
                 timid and proud"
a boy, Mann's boy — and not Bordereau.
Giovane as the Fountain of Youth!

. . . something about Venetian girls, too.
               Having sweet and charming
and very sad, oval faces.
And wasn't there something about
                   an underfed
look? Well, I never thought of them
in those terms . . .

To take a posture — "I quote the principle
                   parts"
"wave-washed steps" (to quote James
to quote myself) seeing this place
           as a getting-away-place, away
from the hardness of plastic edges
           and the sharp surface
of every secure thought I ever had,
is, in itself, a conspiracy

    Left to rifle the situation
I'd hang them all in San Marco
like the French conspirators
             were hanged
after the plot of 1618
             was uncovered . . .
Then console myself with the music
   of Schubert and Miles.
They?

Her face was framed by
                a halo of thick dark hair:
she was no doubt a contessa, (they
        all are!)
    and you could see the distant signs
of the Orient around her African eyes,
            the Middle East
in the slope of her nose.
She was the summation of the human race?
    Her seriousness was Greek.
There was no way to point
        a reckless finger
at any part of her.

In her knit stockings,
            she walks
arm-in-arm with another girl
    — she parts with the friend and
calls back over her shoulder,
                "Ciao, Anna!"

    She is the dama Veneziana
of the 1720s,
                complete with hooped
                    silk skirts
and a black velvet cape
which is attached
            to her jewel-studded crown
and reaches nearly to the floor.
She carries in her left hand
                a gold cross
suspended on a circle
                of pearls.

II

They sit silently in the dark
                    holding hands
watching Jean Marais in *Blas*
     and Lillian Harvey
and Carla Sveva
                    in *Castelli in Aria.*
They?

     and Luchino Visconti's *Senso*
and David Lean's *Tempo d'Estate*
                    and a Volkoff
adventure film
starring Ivan Mosjoukine
     and Max Calandri's *Sangue*
                    a Ca' Foscari.

They seek images
               of their own memories
listen to the emperors
               and to Marco Polo
zigzag mentally through Kublai Khan
     and watch
William Dean Howells swim
               in the Grand Canal.

III

She takes him into "The Rape
                of Europa" —
he takes her by surprise
           by playing the Avocadore
               di Comun.
She delights him as Puttana
   then again as Odalisca.
He scares her as Nobilgiovine
              Veneziano
and again as Cuoco
          of the Hotel Saturnia.
He scares her nearly out
   of her senses
when he does his Compagno
              della Buona Morte
          act.
He is her cavalier-servant.
     He helps her lace
her underclothes,
     to take off her tight
               corset.
The music they live by
         is made for chambers.
He takes her duck hunting
         at the mouth
of Tagliamento, in the winter.
    He puts her up in the best room
at the Palazzo Gritti.
        They got no interest
in Harry's, nor Martini Montgomery.
        In the summer, they fight
off zanzare and spend much time

on the islands.
They go onto the mainland
        Sundays or Saturdays
and drive along Monfalcone
    and through Latisana.
    Once with Bill and Franca,
            they ate the best
spaghetti in butter
                you could ever
                        taste
        in Casale sul Sile

They toasted Carlo Goldoni's
                    humor
    and saw in his home
the only play Picasso
            ever wrote.

IV

He gave the Fascisti salute
               when he stepped off
the plane . . .
                   there would be, I knew —
if nobody else ever knew — an endless
                       Sordello;
and poor "Eleanor" and all
the dream-dreamed Grecian faces
                  I could scare up,
the cries in the nightmares,
     the Acaetes-announcements;
everything you can imagine —
               least of all,
that worn-out, "Hang it all . . ."
               and
and . . . worse! One could get hung
     endlessly up in it all.
I said in my attempt to clear
                 my mind,
     "Goodbye So-shu!"
and I was waiting,
     on my way,
not even mindful of night
                   whisperings:
     "Past we glide!"
There were those
             willing to introduce me
to o.r., but she was too old,
     and therefore
the conversation was likely to be
not worth the trip, but —

on the other hand,
there remained the quest
                    for kissing:
"Kiss me as if you entered gay /
    My heart at some noonday."

The gondolas always
                    repeat always —
cost too much — any year.

I was either a guilty traveller
                    from or to
"glorious Babylon" or else
    I was less wise,
less concerned
                    with these surface effects.

A deep echo of Disraeli,
    fearful of my plight here . . .?
                    at sight of cemetery
lying there in mist, I drew
back, sharing Disraeli's fear.
            Can you imagine yourself
wandering into a late-night-bar
                    in Venice
wearing a mask — even at Carnevale time?

            We bought the papier-mâché
                and covered our faces
        for fun, gambling

on our luck.
    (The Serenissima, in these days,
        would not try us for it —)

    but

poor Disraeli! "I fear I have no title"
        he said,
"to admission within these walls,
                except the privilege
of the season."
            Only in a psychological romance!
But then you try to find a way out!
                or you wait
and listen to Countess Malbrizzi,
    who asks,
            "Shall I tell you
your name?"
and you know
            damned well
if you let her
    you are going to end up
in bed with her, ah, making love,
        or worse!
    And once you are with her,
close to her,
        in her arms, you are obliged
        to not only let her tell you
your name, but to let her melt your snow.
            Mount you?
            Warm you?
As the countess
                she will tell you
she has the power to dream
                you away,
to turn you into a ghost,
                make you
part of the city, fade you.
            And you will be quick
to warn her that you have never had any
    "sympathy with reality."

Then there's Dickens.
            "So we advanced into the ghostly city"
      and Dickens had had no idea
of what he was talking about!
            the proof is that he went on.
". . . a black boat . . ."
                  one of "mournful colours . . ."
      moving
silently through the night

            (I saw them
all day long, mainly — which proves
                  nothing —)

Yet something in you
                  has to go out
to that old boy, Dickens!
            "So we advanced
into the ghostly city" — of
            (death, death, death!)

Poor Dickens!

VI

Nothing in me goes out
                to the stuffy one
who comes over from the Lido because
                        he has to, to
buy some cheap thing or other,
                and resents having to
bump shoulders with the people, nothing,
                absolutely nothing,
whether we're talking about 1921,
                        or 1985: nothing,
nothing, nothing!

Everywhere, you step
                gingerly
to avoid dogshit.
        She was smoking a cigar.
            He was causing a ruckus.
The tourists were beginning
                    to come in greater
numbers. You could easily keep count
            of the big ships
coming in this time
                of year. Flooding
didn't matter.
            Unlike John Evelyn,
I was not constantly surprised.
        I was at home,
as I imagined myself among the best
                            of them!
Them? — Again.
    Poor Dickens, poor Disraeli!

Goosebump weather!
"--Oh, / How beautiful is sunset
when the glow /
of Heaven descends upon a land
like thee,
Thou Paradise of exiles . . ."
I won't say "Italy!"
Damned fool! — Did he never know?

I tried to be patient.

I was not Lord Chesterfield's son
waiting for a letter
from dad. Tightly woven missiles
of moral purity
were never aimed at me.

VII

"Too many gondolas!"
                not ready to bark,
                      "Too much silk,
too much fruit, too much fish,
                too much . . . ! ! ! !"

           I could eat an ice
on the street
              and dress for dinner
and have a cocktail
          and not
in some way, shift personality.
I did not want to ask of Venice:
    "What has become of your . . ."
For me, it still possessed —
                    all . . .
    Browning's worry about
its soul — "Venice spent
    what Venice earned."

VIII

and as the memory of each
                       hard melodramatic word
laced my mind
              I heard (thoughts
of Shelley's Ocean's nursling)
                             plus
the language pitch
           of this
       "woebegone population"

in other words, was this still
such a place? of "blearness
                   of scrofulous children?"
in a landscape of draggletailed
                    pregnant women.
I didn't think so.
    A different enchantment
now held.

IX

There he was, a boy, looking over
                         the canal
at the hostile area with its grandiose
                              structures.
It was years later
             that he thought
it unnatural they locked the gates,
             (closing them in)
                    at night —
prisoners in their own beds.
     Why should he ever want
to go over there?
     The boys threw rocks at them.
Everybody he felt safe with
                    wore yellow hats.
Heathen roughs wore no large O's
             on their breasts.

The day before Dead Day,
            we are on the ship
to Torcello. Happy,
            bright and warm.
Brief and sweet.

Saw contemporary paintings
    at Palazzo dei Diamanti.
    The one of casanova soup
    suited my innocence best.
P. favored the winged crudities.
    Search me!

Went back to San Erasmo
            for the fiesta — this time
it was sunny
    and they had ribs.
Didn't stay for the break-dancing.

Must take the ferry
    from Alberoni to Pellestrina
because
    everybody says we must.

Man scrapes rust from fondamenta
                            rail
morning. Paints it black
    after four.

M.L. came down from France.
        Spent three nights.
            Wonderful, seeing her.

On the Lido again—
        Winter sky. Coffee
outside. Via Negroponte
            & Gran Viale Santa Maria
                            Elisabetta
Girl misunderstands
            my misunderstanding
regarding the lire.
Later, walked on the beach.
            Breeze, sharp green
and gray.

Dreamed about the Festa del Mosto.
    In the dream, stayed for
                        the dancing.
All of it—
        Manifestâzione
        Regata mita
        Spettacolo
        Pemiazione dei
            etc.

To the train station
        to buy the paper.
Lonely and cold, the weary
                    children
of All Western Nations
                sit
on the steps with the birds,
    gazing at the boats
going by on the Grand Canal.
    Backpacks stashed
by their legs.

        They sleep

in the protective coves
        of quiet campi
                and grand old churches.
If Winter is not here yet,
                it's coming—
and fast.

Seagulls scream
        as they circle
the fish market.
            The fishseller
laughs and throws them
                little sardines
or the parts scraped out
        of the larger fish.
They swoop down,
fighting over the gifts.

The gondola riders look up
        insecurely at windows,
not trusting the trip
                    they are on.
In darkness, they drift
        silently along—wildly
drinking wine from the bottle
            and
            slapping
each other's knees.

Smells of fried fish
        and grilled steaks
    at outdoor table
            across from Piazzale Frari.
Italian lessons, anybody?
Signora carries her boots

till she comes
to a puddle. There, she puts
                them on and
walks right through like
    nobody's business.

Girl takes off shoes
    walks barefoot
                through, while
the anarchists come
                to Venice
wearing cool irritation
                like suede boots!

the tour guide has a bright scarf
    pinned to his hat.
The group follows the scarf.

Signora brings the chicken
    back to the butcher,
sticks it under his nose,
        commands him
to smell its rotten odor.
Swirling feather falls
    from sky in front
of the school of birds.
        "When I went back
to America I was shocked
        by the sound of cars."
"Gondola! Gondola!" — the mournful
                call . . .

After the rain, the canal water
        rushes along, tossing
the boats violently against

embankments.
In the afternoon,
    the city is sluggish
with humidity — a heaviness
          made
more of silence than air.

A sudden, hard clear sky!
    My head clears in
        the strong morning light.

Japanese tourists
        armed to the teeth
with cameras go by
      under the window
in a string of gondolas.
          On TV, Japanese
cartoons in Italian —

Graffito — as history:

Yankee Go Home!

TANZ

CLOAX!

RATZ

Terroristi!

Fuk!!

Brigate Rosse!

Il Duce!

Signora sits on chair
    in restaurant, waiting
for hard rolls and creamed coffee.
Her feet do not touch the floor.

Water-level drops low

          in the canal
and the stink rises.
    My knee swells
and the foot shrinks

       and Poe's man
cemented in a wine cellar wall,
    at carnival time, you see
"There is such a thing as being
      too profound.
Truth is not always in a well."

XI

Peggy G's home with its Enchanted Forest
                                    is   open,
hard gray and iron black
                    against the soft pinks
across the Grand Canal . . .
            Empire of Light
            Angel of the Citadel
The place itself is Alchemy.
                You can go out
                in the stone yard
                        and sit and see
                    the boats go by.
The Zoomorphic couple will not
            come out and join ya!
They are hopelessly entangled
            in their own tentacles.

Also —
        go, then, to "feast the eyes"
            on the golds and silvers,
                the reds and blues
Salome dancing with Herod's head
                held above her own —
Shapely, shark-quick
            and not a drop of blood
                            spilled
on her mink.
            I guess it's mink
(and see him
            before he's beheaded
interrogating the Three Magi
            as they plead and dance
on their toes

without upsetting
          their crowns).

And —
    touch the brilliant rough surface
of yellow gold behind Madonna Nicopeia's
          black-covered head.
She holds the c.c. against her stomach.
    He's a piece of wood held
        like a wood block —
a little old man
          whose red lips know no smile,
whose eyes are more untrusting
               than his mother's.

Follow him, grown,
               as he rides a jackass
with the face of an upstate farmer
               into the City.

Outside —
        a boat on spaghetti-waves
bringing back the Body —
          stiff and in skullcap,
very holy-looking, this body . . .
               Patron, patron!
Sailors lower the white sails
        as the vessel nears
the lagoons . . .

You may then want to go
          back inside.
They go.
We go.
She goes back inside.
    I go back inside

and there is Noah,
poor Noah, sending out the raven
and the dove
from both hands held together.
You will like his sturdy face.
You can tell he trusts
the birds.
You may notice his hands:
small, with the fingers you expect
a twelve-year-old girl
to scratch herself
with.

And since you're there,
touch the surface
of La Pala d'Ora
in the Basilica —
rubies
emeralds
sapphires
pearls
laid in networks of gold.

Then go across the city
by way of
the small calli
to look up
at the Assumption
(retouched, I think)
with a Venetian sky
just behind the earth-bound
reachers & worshippers
All, except the messenger-man, looking
up
at the cherub-paced heavens.
It's enough for one day.

XII

The theme of Carnevale is a secret
                this year.
You have to guess; play the game!
          The mystery is the main
                    thing.
You do see various variations
         of classic figures:
Doctor of the Plague
Bauta
      Rotunello — in baggy pants
        carrying a string
        of sausage
          — from Roma,
of course.
      And kindly Bertolado
        on donkey-back.
    He comes here
from Bologna . . . with:
      Dottore Balanzone —
        serious-minded fella,
        this one.
    He spills red wine
    on his white collar;
takes his cape off & places it over
           a puddle
so that native Signora Rosawra
may cross. Others —
    Lucinda, Isabella,
      Flaminia —
follow her lead.
    Poor Dottore Balanzone!
    (Meanwhile, nobody

puts down a cape
        for Colombina
to cross the puddle on.
            Faggiolino suggests
she take off her apron
            and spread it over
                    the water.
The crowd laughs.)
            And those from Bergamo —
Brighetta, first.
    A pirate with a long twisted
                        nose
and a dagger in his belt
    he'll cut your throat
                    for two hundred lire
                    or less.
And Scapino,
        in blue. Well dressed.
                Yank his cape.
    And Messetino!
        pluck the strings
                of his guitar!
    Dance with him, in
his red balloon outfit.

Arlecchino —
    harlequin, spotted
and sporting the feather
            plucked
from the tail of a green-headed
                        duck
that has come on the wind
                down
from Siberia, for the winter.
        Introduced by Goldoni

himself,
the spectators cheer.
Only one Bronx cheer.
That, overall, is a good reception.

Now,
Bagottino
in black mask
and white shirt & pants.
Meo Squacquera (from
Calabria) with sword
dangling
from his hip — mouth
free of the long-nosed
mask — cap flying behind him
as he dances violently
to a music imported
all the way from China.
Then to music from Spain,
where the bulls
used to come from.

Proud — unmasked — Lelio,
native, leans on his cane,
watching
Bagottino & Meo S. make fools
of themselves.

Little Captain Spaventa (of
Liguria)
struts about
with hands on his hips,
cape dragging
feathers in his band
so long they dangle

in his face.

Playful boy yanks Gianduia's pigtail
        and he loses his Torino cool,
tries to catch the culprit
                but the kid is
        a break-dancer
who has developed
        a running-ability
        equal to the East Bronx's
                hellishness.

You will take a sip
                of the brisk wine
Meneghino offers you.
He comes from Milano
        with the kegs on his donkey.
He drinks to your health.
You had better drink
                to his, too.

If you meet Patacca
        in a dark calle,
walk sideways, and pray.
And these ones from the South—

                Pasquino
                Pulcinella
                Scaramuccia

What can I say?
        Dance barefoot with one,
        tap your walking-stick
                with the other,
        exchange knickers

with still
another!
Clown! Snatch a skullcap
from a dwarf!
And the natives —
Pantalone,
bearded & caped
Florindo —
like a French madam
in riding britches — carrying
a proper crop!

And the others —
Stenterello:
funny-faced guy
in orange vest
under his blue suit.
Firenze accent . . .

Tartaglia — of Campania.
Dance with him
at the ball.
His yellow stripes
will dazzle
you.
Dance with Pugantino
balanced
on your shoulder.
He will enjoy
the ride.

Then when the formal parade
has passed
you realize how relaxed everybody is.
Nobody pushes.

But nowadays this is the
                    way it is:
Under a flimsy pink parasole,
        held above his head,
he walks proudly
        through the campo—
    a black silk mask
covers his face.
        Tucked beneath his silk
hat, and covering the sides
    of his face, a piece of old lace:
unless you know his walk
        you cannot guess.
He holds the hand
        of a clown
with a big red nose.
        You snap
their picture.

        Carnevale is not
yet defeated, though
        it's raining cats
and—

XIII

Once you are in the Palazzo Ducale
       do not expect
anybody to tell you how to get out.
                  Stuck
you will be.
Stay, you must.

             You will not be
reborn here.
The San Marco flood
       will not wash you
out, back into the canal.
You will not drift
       out, dreamlike
rolling in mud,
       under a sand-black sky,
while the whole piazza
       glows dimly red—
   Once it's clear the storm
is coming.
        When it hits, watch out!

XIV

Little places.

       Corte Stella.
    White sheets hanging
          on clotheslines.
   Flowerpots
      inside barred windows.
Broom propped against wall.

       Rio de San Barnaba.
   Gondolas.
         One half-sunken,
filled with snow.
  On the other side, little boats —
sleeping birds.
       Their bodies reflected
upside-down in the water.

       Rio Terrà dei Catecumeni.
   Windows covered
with a profusion of blooming vines.
         Winter sunlight
   in Spring.

XV

PG? The sister, the nose, the money.
    But then—hey!—most people
            have silly lives,
as silly as hers.
        The long early stretch
            without work—then
art collecting. It's the only thing
    you can do most of the time,
         (Faulkner).

We went (what a way to begin!)
    to see Eleonora,
        dramatic Eleonora,
    sitting forward
        on the edge
of her chair   there in the dark
              room,
    fully dressed, in fact
overly dressed, bejewelled,
        but sad, sad
in Asolo.

    with Bill and Franca again,
early Spring . . .
You know those sudden thunderstorms
        in Venice. And sun
again so . . . We escaped Venice
    and the tourists coming in, in
the manner of real Venetians,
      (they were, anyway—
she certainly, from the beginning)
        went
to visit the great Poet.

First, in the yard
I lost myself
                climbing
                    into the hedges
                        hanging
from the wall
        of his grand villa.
Bees nearly stung me to death.
    Colder, later, inside
                than out in the sun
with the mountains behind.
            ("Did you say pasta
                    or basta?")
The great Poet wasn't home but
            the caretaker let us in,
and we studied the furniture,
                the stone floor,
            the scenes of his life
                        left
in the things possessing him,
            his rare books,
            his rarer manuscripts,
            his priceless great chair.
Leaving, in the yard
            we were caught in the thunder
of an approaching storm. Rain came like bullets.
To escape, we hid under the hanging vines.

In the car going back
                Franca sang the poet's
                            songs
remembered from liceo
            when she was made by the maestro
                                di scuola
                    to sing them.

XVI

We climbed the hill to the carriages
    but saw how the royal family,
        down there behind us,
drove in, slowly,
feeling great and proud,
    as they approached the castle, yet—
going on, up and in,
    we laughed at the funny ones,
and admired them all,
    all of them with wheels.
It was a day, an outing,
    and the food (I splashed
snail sauce in my own eye!)
        was worth it,
and the ambience was all of it.
After the big Easter feast,
    in a crowded room,
we went out and sat on the grass
    and I sketched
the village in the valley below
           with
its mountains ranged beyond.
But all of this was before
    the carriages: queen's,
        king's, gent's.
Then we came down,
    bellies full still, and feeling
grand and humble, not minding
    not getting into the villa
    here at Maser
where Veronese painted the walls
    with hunting scenes

for the wealthy family, not minding
and
minding a little bit anyway,
sad and happy,
fretful and calm,
we drove back
to Venice, our city of canals.

XVII

in Salute again.
        This time, did not feel
burning from arrows shot
        into neck, chest, stomach, thigh.
I bled though, but not much.
   To fight pain I kept
        in view the woman
across the room; she's from Orante.
Her passion is sad.
   Distraction is good for pain.

Out to Torcello again.
        Hard Spring! Light
high and sharp, higher noon clear
   with shadows deeper
        than direct,
and beneath us—hey!—the Antichrist
   on his throne
holding the c.c. on his lap.
   Not exactly the way I
        remember
it, the fire
and angels poking heads
   you might have thought
good or at least worthy
       of ascent,
         down
into the volcano.
   Out there there are levels:
      skull bones (finished)
      people waiting (to burn)
      the half-burned

Lucifero in his inferno!
The woman from Assunta
at the other end, trapped
in mosaic, unable to move
even
if she wanted to
lift a finger —

The light in San Giorgio dei Greci
is not the best yet
you reach up through it
to touch The Passion
in the Orthodox manner
with its seventeenth century
red gold yellow-gold, but
your fingers fumble instead
upon the eyelids
and across her nose, blindly
guessing appearance.
Faith in art restored,
you go next door
and into the arms
of the woman of Hodigitria.
As though you really were her child,
she makes you
look
toward the camera, tickles your belly,
tries to make you smile
but too many centuries
of suffering the sins
of Judeo-Christian heartbeat
have turned your little head
and its quite odd face
to metal quickly painted brown.
Here in Ellenico

there is a stillness, tender
    but not soft enough to soften
your hardness.
    Your fingers, chubby and little,
        play
with the stone-hard creases
        in her dry-blood
          red robe.

XVIII

You set out on a morning bright
    for the guild,
as though you were an invited guest,
    about to take part
in some important civic discussion,
  and
who knows,
    you might do just that,
       after all.
Here in the Scuola Dalmata, the caretaker
      mumbles to himself
pacing between the card rack
  and the entrance to the upstairs
         room.
  Darkness is cold, and the only light
comes from the static voice
    of Carpaccio's . . .
George is calm, almost bored
   as he drives the spear
  into the neck of The Uncontrollable Forces
      of Nature.
You know he is almost too late.
   Look! Look at the destruction
   he's already responsible for.
   Yet you see among the half-eaten bodies
     there are skullbones
of other animals
so you know you are not up against
    a discriminating beast!
His fire, like the fires of Hell
   heating the furnace of Heaven,
    at the Ellenico, is also ironic

George could not be more
                      connected
to the dragon than he is
          by the straightness
of his spear. The serenity behind him
            in the land and the sky,
even in the straight still trees,
      and the bright little buildings,
and in the calm water of the river,
      (more a mediaeval Tuscan *virtù*
      than Venetian!)
      are as much
                  connected
to the dramatic turn of events,
                        the sharp,
abrupt lines, created by George's horse,
                  the spear, as to
the bleeding dragon,
                  George himself.
And this is where the discussion
                        begins.

But what you are not aware of
                        is this:
a lion has followed a man
                  into
the scuola and when you turn
      and see this for yourself
you know why the others gathered here
      are running in every direction —
some upstairs,
      others towards the door.
The Lion-Man is old. He uses a walking stick
                        to walk
      You see the caretaker's fear grow

as he trembles.
A group of monks
          that has just entered
     turn
and return to the fondamenta.

XIX

"There was romance. There is always
                    romance,"
said Mrs. Douglas in *The Valley*
              of Fear.
              Fear and romance merge in the sun-
flower: spread across the red-inked view
              of romance,
mackerel Mediterranean, this sense
                    of sea-swept clouds
just off coast, beyond Laguna!
              Romantic sails out
past glass factories,
              from oil-covered bridges,
beneath which the stream
              shows the evening sun exaggerated
and horizon roofs red
              as geranium blossoms — so
                    romantic!
I have here a view of the sea lighted
                    and tossed
with yellow light of early August.
     (The guy from across the canal
              probably has his sailboat out
              on a day like this, tossing
in the weeping wind.)

XX

Beckett didn't come here, at least
        not on the same day Christopher
Marlowe chose a darkness in the tower—no,
                        campo; to music
by S. (He's over there on the island now.)
    But it's more b's than c's I'm talking
                        about.
Not Burgess though. Venice has nothing
        to offer that is
not already in the spirit,
                already . . . A lot
  can be done with doubt.
                Byzantines doubted not.
Beloved ones doubted not.
    Beheld ones doubted not.
            Desdemona and Mann doubted.
The dama Veneziana came grandly
                into the campo.
    No doubt.
Those who raped Europe had no doubt
                in their own Thrust.
    People in Harry's Bar
seem to doubt nothing on earth;
                they lift
their glasses to their lips
                with dead certainty.

XXI

. . . out to Vignole —
      where algae grows
thick black-green
              along the canal wall
  by the little wood bridge
where the fountain is . . .
          water
low and still and the mosquitos
   in profusive growth
         on slime
here . . . and grass
   tough and tall along path —

   a wonderful wilderness!

a channel black dog
     big as a donkey
watches our progress through
the backyard toward Trattoria
     alle Vignole,
where two old women
         wash fish and caution
piano piano . . .

   — While waiting for ribs
on grill, we kick our way
Down to the shore where
     fishing boats are moored
in stillness and a fat old woman
   in a red bathing suit
     and a little fat girl
in one blue with white flowers

hold their hands
                over their eyes
        shielding them from the sun
to see better
            these strangers—here
    where strangers are rare . . .

The shirtless men with their big red
    bellies, sun themselves
    after lunch—
        smoking and drinking coffee . . .

XXII

In a blazing sunset
                    the gondola
moves silently along
                    the surface
of the lagoon, like somebody
                    trying to pull something
over on a sleeping person.

Green ducks fly up
                    against the light,
electric as shock,
                    from some invisible crevice,
and they are caught
                    in midair
by my own wonderment,
                    and remain bright
    as dandelions
and as tentative as cats
                    on the fondamenta
after a storm.

XXIII

and the single reality
    of the closely lined
buildings, casa after casa,
        reflected,
like a young man's convictions
                (shaky,
upside-down, blurred,
        like yellow and white
flesh, are somehow steady
        and understood, sure
as the hand of a housekeeper
            who has been
with the family
        for nearly a century)
is a reality uncelebrated
                except
in bad photographs
        by determined tourists.

That's how important
                the long dark point
of this simplicity is.
    Is there progress?
Do you mean, uh, toward recognition?
        Yes, eyes about to open to
the occasion, and it is
        bending with the wind,
where everything suddenly
            might be seen,
as it breaks with a snap,
            and the joy of it,
transformed as understanding,

            stays on clearly
centered and smelling
              like sap
from a young branch.

XXIV

Yes, we are moving into Fall.
        It is an important blue-
green occasion, when the buildings
          throb upside-down
in the Grand Canal,
      like a promise
made by a child
       to another child,
    as difficult to hold
as an umbrella in high wind,
       and as difficult to keep,
though it remains, unkeepable
        as it may be, it stays,
hard and unchanging
        in the disfigured surface
of time. Nothing else
         matters more
than the light, sparked as that light
          from rowing,
and that light from blades,
       and I could go on . . .

XXV

See that stern castle? It was once
    a great old whorehouse.
Now, all alone, empty,
      closed for centuries,
no boat anchor; it is unmarked.
    It might even in some ways
be seen as a lonely casa
      in a graveyard,
for over here, on this side
      not far from the cemetery
the merry daylight of death
      is always waving
its tear-stained flag.
          Still,
vain, dreamy, defamed
      and the victim
of a lost fortune, this place
      is a sentry
to the flesh-grinding profits
      of the pirates
who smiled beautifully
    and lived filled with noise
while trying to avoid the Bridge
      of Sighs.
Stout women
    once leaned out
of those windows
      purring like motorboats,
        waving to sailors
passing below
      in narrow boats,
    in long, slender, nice-looking

boats.
If we were to glide by
          now,
                    very close to the dock,
we would hear the echoes
          of an enchanted though bruised
                              life;
peculiar in its solitude, while
          thoughtless
in its sentimental enthusiasm.
                    As we go by
out here, far from it,
                    without moral peril,
     in our vaporetto,
                    we are travellers,
far too far from those decorated windows
          to catch even the ghosts
of kisses thrown,
          for centuries, down
from them.

XXVI

Badly sick in bed
    but only for a quick week,
I drew a picture
      of my own stomach
to show the doctor
      next time.
In this, our bedroom,
    with no Turner-view
of the Grand Canal.
It was not a tomb, floating
      all the way out
to the sea. Commander
    of profound stillness,
the bed became my workshop.
    I became familiar
with the ceiling also: gaudy
      decorations in gold
and white, pale green,
      sick yellow,
feverish pink. Hangover silver.
    I could go on, like Rilke
about blue. My illness
    was no romantic comedy,
though it was crowded
      with opera
figures pretending
    to take real life
very seriously. All there
      on my bed, spread
out before me, pretending
    to be print
on the pages of books,

in magazines.
And P. had to do all
             the shopping alone,
       and bring up the water,
                    and talk
Italian with anybody
          who rang the doorbell.
But, like I said, the week
             went swiftly, like
a bleeding sunset
          at that time of year.

XXVII

Saturday.
        On the ship about to sail
for Pellestrina.
      "Arrivederci! Arrivederci!"
        I thought of Hemingway:
          "She used to be the queen
          of the seas and the people are
          very tough and they give less
          of a good goddamn about things
          than almost anybody you'll meet.
          It's a tougher town than Cheyenne
          when you really know it, and
          everybody is very polite."
   to those waving goodbye
to Saturday relatives, "Arrivederci!"
   And we moved out,
        among fishing boats
and cargo vessels,
       sprinkled in the south lagoon.
A police boat speeds by.
     As terra firma recedes,
P. and I go out
       on the back upper deck,
to watch Venice change.

XXVIII

The old woman comes
        along our fondamenta,
                Tolentini,
every morning around nine,
            dropping sardines
along the way, with
        the cats trailing her,
eating the fish. Lucky,
           these cats.
Those in the Campo San Vitale
              suffer,
especially when the construction
            workers
are not working
        on Ponte dell' Accademia.
And when it's finished?
        It is Winter, already.

XXIX

Shy. She keeps a stiff
                upper lip,
dresses like a 12-year-old
        boy forced to be clean
        — with tie and polished shoes —
in some sedate military academy.
                Proud. She works hard
at hiding her total self-interest.
She pants like a drill-sergeant,
folds her hands across
                her stomach, speaks
out the side of her mouth
                like a guy (to the one behind him)
in an Attica line
        on the way to license-plate making.
— Her eyes. Her eyes are sharp
        and clear. She is in control.
        Her brushes are clean.
Her canvases are stretched
        with the unmistakable tightness
                of a firm wind
        against a sail
                in sun on distant
                        Mare Adriatico.
She is ready.
Exhibition gallery. Her show
        opens. She stands
at the entrance greeting
                the guests. They come
from the expected philosophical positions
but the unexpected drifters
        please her most — even

if they are stupid,
        they mean her
            no harm.
The others she knows
            too well.

XXX

They cut down the last tree
              on the campo
                        where I sit
near the old boatyard at San Trovaso.
                The birds also miss it:
    they fly into the space
where it once stood and sink,
                as though
          in quicksand.
I can now see the path,
                   church
    and castle. But
did I need to?
         Rain now
falls hard to the ground,
    with no leaves or limbs
               to pause on.
Yet, when did Venice
              seriously
    need trees or gardens
                  not secretly
kept behind stone walls?

XXXI

The canal, this one,
                was dug at the turn
of the century. Beneath
          the fondamenta
              are the logs
and mud
     of an incredible handshake.
No sharp shadows
          are left. Buildings,
     dynamic yet so elusive
they might be illusions,
             in winter light.
Space unnatural?
           Over on the main-
land, at Mestre,
        a redundant green
              wind, high
whipping dresses
         against thighs. Cemented
drain carries water
        on down
toward the library,
       but not quite that far.

XXXII

I was back in Longmont, Colorado
        one night
            yet, my body
stayed in bed in Venice.
        As I drove
              down
        the main street, I saw
gray, fashionable hotels
           right alongside
feed stores, hardware stores.
    The sun was almost
           completely down
and the sky straight
        ahead, was full of blue
cavalry riders in lemon-
                colored uniforms.
Their horses galloped
           across a beach stretch
        of banana fish.
I smelled the lagoon.
           No question about those odors.
I stopped at the light.
    The Venetian Lagoon Company boat,
        on a trailer, stopped
by my Ford. I looked
        at the driver.
He had some good advice
        on where I could buy
           tourist junk.
No thanks.
        It took them ten minutes
at the Danieli Royale

to find my reservation.
While waiting,
        I scrutinized the people
    in the lobby: mostly
Italian cowboys, farmers
            with red necks, guys
sure they made the right decision
        when they quit high school
to become men.
            Twenty minutes later,
    on the fondamenta
            and walking toward
                a sky
now onyx, filled with jujitsu
                arm-swings
my sails furled, my mainstay
            flew to pieces.
Some kind of helmsman,
            I ran along
an embankment,
            walked two blocks
down Riva degli Schiavoni,
            past the elegant ones
    out for a stroll,
mingling with the cowpokes
        and innocent people
            on cheap tours,
trying their best to remain
        who they were,
            in the face of
                this, the
oldest Republic.
            Gondoliers
steered their gondolas
            along the asphalt,

hawking, barking,
      singing sweetly,
            waving to the girls
of Longmont.

XXXIII

and always, *always!* those
                closed shutters!
so early, against —
        not just the cold fog —
the clammy night (because
                everyone
is out strolling).
        We learned
          to close ours
early, too: it was
        obviously
considered rude not to.
              Island people,
the eighteenth-century
          expert
insisted, are beautiful
            thieves.
Look at San Marco!
        Thieves whisper
best behind closed shutters.
   Lovers are more
        alone there.

XXXIV

Spring truly is here.
          The upward swing of feeling
                    matches the day.
You both place offerings
          on the graves of pirates
at San Michele.

In the silence you hear
          political whisperings,
coming across the lagoon
          from the sea,
                    which is still,
like a killer crouched behind
                    your front door;
          but only half the time.
     Maybe, just maybe,
          from as far away
as Leningrad or Washington,
          Spring is whispering
political thoughts.

Meanwhile
          you try to hold,
     the future
to maintain
          a balance
                    of your own
strength and pulse together,
          while listening to the voices.
     You know they touch you
but exactly how,
          and why, leaves you

with the dumb question:
   "Can you tell
who's coming by
      the sound of the walking?"

You seek distraction
    by exploring

      Como
      Bergamo
      Cortina d'Ampezzo

by seeking out Adriana Ivancich,
   and by getting friends
to write to the officials
    urging them to
decorate you
      with an honor,
perhaps the Cavaliere
    di Gran Croce al Merito
so that you can strut
   through the city,
     cross every bridge
at least once,
   and proclaim the city
your own personal playground.
      This distraction
you realize,
    from the beginning,
      may be your own
way of sandpapering
     the rough surface
of your own political
     consciousness.
And once it is smooth,
    then what?

XXXV

Alone, I went into that special
                    little windowless bar
near Rialto market,
          said to be the oldest
                    of its kind
in Venice; ordered,
          with exaggerated ease,
     (like an exhibitionistic
                    bullfighter
waving his *muleta* unnecessarily,)
          a tocai and began
to eat the sausages
          from the tray,
     just like the regulars do,
attempting to feel
               Venetian.
It didn't work.
          The fish at the end
of the line finishes himself
               by pulling
against it. The bartender
          overcharged me
as though I were a tourist.
               Had I not lived here
a long, long time?
          Then I returned
               a week later,
quite by chance,
               with A.,
     who's very, very Venetian,
          classy and quick,
We had our tocai

and sausage together.
Two fishermen in the alley
                    outside
    were laughing happily.
The bartender gave me,
            like a present,
his biggest smile.
            I felt the Great Blue
River running through my veins.
            I was a way
        I had never been before.
A., and I had our tocai again,
                and the bartender
insisted we have thirds
            on him.
    With a light head,
            and happy at noon,
I walked home the busy way,
        and found P.
            making lunch.

XXXVI

The time sequence may not be
                              correct
but what happens, what matters
          is the "soap smooth"
                         connection,
emotionally speaking. Isn't that
                              true?
So, in July,
          at the Festa
                    del Redentore,
with the Doctor of the Plague,
               in black,
          wearing a wide-brimmed black
                              hat,
and the mask with its pelican-
                         like
nose, at my side;
          I see myself,
all this time
                    later,
          dressing in the first-floor
hotel room,
          ready, or getting ready
                    to go out
with the others
          walking the fondamentae
and piazzettae and rio terrae
               and maybe stopping
at the wooden bridge,
               Ponte dell'Accademia
     to look down the canal
before going on to the old Biennale

                                        galleries.
I am wearing my summer blue
                                        suit,
            bought in Paris.
P. is dressed in her summer pink.
            We are figures
fastened to a great moment.
            We enter some piazza,
and everybody looks
            at all of us
      go by.
Still, there are others
  and they are waiting
      for us
at a café near Ca' D' Oro,
      where we have sat
in the mornings
      having coffee with rolls.

XXXVII

A Venice dream of the mainland:
      shocked out of night
by morning, waking
        on a duck stream,
my tongue dry, swollen,
      as from the air
  in a torture room, I stand up
in sleep, looking up
      at the zinc dome
    of the sky, I try counting
        the flock
of geese exploding overhead.
      I had about as much luck
doing that
      as I had trying
to restrain the mad dogs
        barking
at them: running upstream.
      Then I woke to the sirens
of acqua alta and the dragons
      known very well
to be reality.

XXXVIII

We drove over to Padova.

The students built a platform
    for G. to lecture from
so they could hear him better.
    I stood on it.
But couldn't get anybody's
                        attention.

I am in charge
    of the trapdoor.
The graverobbers know
        me.
    The hunters bring the
              gaunt boar
    and the wild dogs,
and the farmers
    the sheep.
Horses are too large.
    At all times
    I keep a carcass
available . . .
        on the floor
in case the officials
    should come
into the room
  of our anatomy lessons
(we can easily drop the corpse—
              to switch—
through the trap to conceal it).

So far no student

                has leaked
our secret: it is for
                        the good
of humanity. It is
amazing how well
            they all realize it,
and even give presents,
                on holy days,
to the families
        of the graverobbers.
They are good boys, all 200,
        and at least
                        eight
will become great
                doctors,
I bet you . . .

XXXIX

The storm had no evil intentions.
                    We knew that,
and that
                    it denied its own name.
Pure wind came, from over
                    San Giorgio,
        once a place of skulls,
and we crawled
                    into the traghetto
hovering like starving dogs
                    across the Ice Age.
We could not locate
                    the exact place
of frostbite, out of season
                    because
the message from our brains
            no longer connected
to the tips of our fingers.
                    The storm
renamed the calli and canals.
    The mind froze
to the degree it could not
                    recollect
the names each of us had
                    before,
leaving us
            as stems without buds.
The storm was not here
                    to say,
You have transgressed,
                    Venice must sink,
pay for ill intentions. No,

it spoke another language:
that of warm, glacial sheets
far out of rhythm with any
frigid texture of meaning.
It made only gestures,
lashing out at San Giorgio
with as much force as it whipped
against
La Giudecca, in its loneliness
width and repose.
Then it pointed to its mouth
(like some horrible god-devil,
begging or demanding,
it seemed), where there was no tongue.

XL

Sitting here at our table
        in front of the coffee shop
                in Chioverate
      de Simon
with the closed hotel
        adjacent the casa
at the end (the one I drew)
      where the shadows
           seem tangible
as hieroglyphic tablets,
           I feel
the utter quarry-like surface
        of this Spring
(or is it already Summer?)
          as hidden relief
   from the cruel theatre
      that passed itself off
as Winter. Even the strike
   today, with shops closed,
and having to resort to canned goods
      for lunch
and possibly dinner,
     is no greater bother
          than the
Jacobin winds rushing
     between these buildings,
      or the sirocco from the desert
of North Africa. This day, blue
     and free of paranoia,
   makes up for the malicious chill
that hung over us so long, wrenching us
    apart

                    from ourselves,
or the best of ourselves.
                    I know
the Adriatic is still
                    out there; and so
be it. Marinetti was so, so wrong:
                    Venice should not be
                        destroyed.
Not on purpose (it will go
            down soon enough),
    and at worst we will remember
only the nosy thieves
        and witty pirates,
as we gaze at the lagoon
        from the factory town,
                            Mestre.
And will the Socialist
        and the Christian Democrat
            finally shake hands
as she sinks?

XLI

They had just arrived.
        He was about to write
a long poem on Venice
            she was going
to paint up a storm.
        They came like a couple
           dragging
a dead horse.
        We took them
    to the terrace
        of the Palazzo Gritti
for drinks
        and pointed out the windows
of Hemingway's suite
           just above us.
They were impressed,
      being literary snobs.
    Then looking at the gondoliers
      standing,
      rowing
their gondolas as though
      they were participants
in the Regata Storica,
      as if everything depended
         on winning,
she said, "My, my
      how romantic!" and
I thought of Mario, the gondolier,
      our friend,
        who worked nights
mostly, and whose smile
      was like a swinging door

         held opened
with a lot of light
      coming from inside,
and I thought
    of Mario when he was angry,
        his flailings,
his grunts, his tipsiness
    (for he was never drunk!)
      and I remembered
the trip to Chioggia,
       on the big ship,
   the crowds, the sun,
      the children screaming,
and there was Mario
       with his family, going
  to visit relatives,
     out of his zanzara darkness . . .
no longer in need of his night
         vision,

insisting that we join them . . .

XLII

Any excuse for a celebration?
    Excitement cannot be manufactured
        and held up to the light
like plastic flowers.
        Yet, the invention
of Vogalonga was not unlike
    that of fine columns, signed
        and dated.
May 8th. We got a good spot
        on the Lido
near the middle. Going by
        were more boats
        than I could count.
They'd started, you know,
    at that place
where the Grand Canal touches
        Riva degli Schiavoni,
    and moved toward San Giorgio.
There, you can hear the cannon
        go off, but
we chose not to deal with the crowd.
    Boom! Boom!
        There, that's loud
enough for me. I felt a rush.
    They were moving with a grace
as tangible as the lines
    on that triumphal dome
        of San Giovanni
at Macerata, toward Malamocco,
    that "charming village,"
    as they say,
where the oarsmen will be fed

                    and celebrated.
Some, of course, will cheat—
                have, already!—
                    by taking a short-
cut to the finish, but
                the main fun is not spoiled,
as the balmy winds
                    of the sirocco
        push the vessels
                        along.
I know, everybody said it was best
                to see it from its
beginning. Prince Charles
        and Princess Diana
                were there. All
the more reason to seek
                another spot.
And once they passed
            we took the vaporetto back
to Venice and had coffee
                at the Canale di Cannaregio,
where the oarsmen would pass
                                again,
on their way back
                to the Grand Canal.

XLIII

In the hidden garden
        you force perspective
                on us
when you push us to flowers
        where flowers are
already crowded,
        losing their aromatic
ability to whisper names,
        names like

                Miranda
                Luigi
                Orlando
                Pasquale
                Valentino

or kick back at us,
        creatures
no stranger than they,
        in groves
    along the stone fence,
like this, here
        in warm lagoon air,
                rain-wet
like the rooftops
    beneath which we spend
        most of our time.
But your garden is special.
                You force us to stand
firmly
        against the only space
            your flowers have left,

while we, sporeless,
                    rootless,
            seasonless, have other
options. Why then, do we weep
        before these flowers?
Let's gather their camphor scent
        with their roughness
and stickiness, to our bosoms.
                If you have a camera,
click fast, because we are
            about to move on
and may not return
                for a long time.

XLIV

(Envoi)

. . . and when we saw the slides,
        the perspective!

In the little red Fiat
        called Junior, we drove
from the Veneto down
                to Cassino.
Nine hours. In the morning
        climbed up to the rebuilt
                monastery —

Up here on Monte Sant'Angelo
        the basilica to Michael

a procession of cure-seekers
        carrying olive branches
                coming toward the church
from a big blue bus with silver fenders
                and Goodyear tires.

a red donkey cart,
        a red car,
        a woman in red . . .
            but those bread-eaters,
                peasants
with bent backs
        hobbling up the narrow
                sidewalk,
and coming up
        on the big glossy blue buses
        all

all
             mournful, worshipful, intent
on prayer, seeking cures —
                    and stumbling down
the dungeon steps
                    with them
                              deep
into Saint Michael's sanctuary
gave me both a sense of shame
                    and awe,
I clung to the wall,
                    so overpowering
and sincere was their faith
                    and its expression.
They made offerings.
             They came with sores.
They were the aged, close to death.
             They came with incurable diseases.
                    (Perhaps they spread
                              their diseases
                                    among themselves.)
They came: busload after busload.
                    (Probably first time
                              off the farm.)
They came. (And years — centuries! — ago
             a group of sheepkeepers took refuge here
and were protected from The Enemy
                    by the saint . . .)
                    So they still come.

in Rialto at Vietri
             you see the sea all the way.
       First the sea.
             Then the sea!
Salerno with her history

is now also one dirty street
one smelly alley
            after another, but San Benedetto
has not forsaken the dirtiest ditch.
            You can drive the narrow winding road —
                  from Vietri
            and see Ravello.
It was raining & the road was narrow
      This is the problem
                  with this road:
            and the drivers
                  drive like madmen,
maybe they are.
            I come around the curve
like a man who simply wants to live
            (this other guy
comes around like a man
                  who expects too much —)

. . . at Paestum
            birds nest high
in the basilica beams
      where moss and buffalo grass grow
from cracks in Hera's honor.
                  Here at the base
                  of Neptune's Temple
I catch an angle with large
                        black tree
in foreground; you'd love it!
      Gymnasium. A Chinese artist sketching it.
      Amphitheatre Square. Italian kids
                  yucking it up. Sunday
before noon. Lunch, the reward
            for boredom. At Paestrum
a priest and two nuns

herd the children
toward the Roman building
north of the Athenaion. We squat
in the shade
till the legs are ready
to move again . . . again we move.
Not a picnic ground, yet
they bring their sandwiches
and corked wine.
The guards will not notice.
Greasy paper
in the Italic Temple . . .

we walk along the wall
of the town.
Sky? hot metal. No hat.
Shadows are directly under

things.

Back to the red Fiat.

"Whatta ya say when ya're in Pompeii?"
You say, Which way?
Drove nearly to the top
of the volcano first
but the red dragon got stuck
in the ash and started sliding
down
so we went to the excavations
and watched the birds bathe
in the bird bath. Parrots, really.
Then the positions
English gents laugh
at, making mental notes to copy.
Why are the men all dark
and the buxom women

all, so pink?

So, one can buy the notion
              that it was simply
        the way . . .
                    (Un) fortune —? Really,
the correct word
              when one thinks of
                    hot lava
pouring down . . . encasing everything
                    and a dumb guidebook
says, "The good fortune was."

The houses —
              in the houses of . . .
well, first Julia Felix's Hotel.
                    There, we stayed
                    and dined in grand fashion.
My wife pressed a flower
                    between the pages
        of the map. Deep purple.
Julia's garden, too, was grand.
                    We walked about in it.
        Once I stayed at Sittius's Inn.
                    Didn't get first-class
treatment. No Albergo di Sittius
                    for me, ever again!
        The "for rent" sign there
              was always up.
At Julia's? Rarely!

In the House of the Bear
              the mosaic
in the entrance framed our pause;
In the House of Cornelius Rufus

we got wet from the steam
coming from across the street
            where bathers
                        had no regard
for anything but their own
        pleasure and pain;
In the House of the Faun
        we heard the unexpected whisperings
of the goddess Fortuna Augusta.

She really was arrogant about
        her claim that only the "best people"
                came
to her little village ("it's not
        the quantity that counts
                        here,
it's the quality").